EVERYTHING YOU NEED TO KNOW TO DO IT RIGHT, SMART AND PROFITABLY

With over 500,000 new books hitting the market every year, how do you make yours stand out so casual browsers become committed buyers? Ellen Reid knows, and she shares what she's learned in her stellar career of creating award-winning books for authors.

Have no illusions; as with anything of quality, it's going to cost you to do it right. However, if you were going to start a new business, you'd want to save money but you wouldn't cut corners on the important things. *Putting Your Best Book Forward* tells you where to spend and how to save.

The book takes you right into today's book business and:

- Describes the self-publishing process so you can see what you might do yourself and where professionals might serve you best (This is different for each author).
- Guides you in how to work with the individuals you hire so you get the greatest benefit from their services.
- Provides pointers on how to look at your specific situation so you can confidently make the choices for producing a book that will best serve your objectives.

If you have a manuscript and want to get it into print, when you finish this book you will know how to do it right, how to do it smart and how to do it so you will be in the best position to prosper in a growing and evolving industry.

I0807975

About the Author

Ellen Reid may not have been the very first Book Shepherd, howevershe is definitely right up at the front of this very small pack. She has distinguished herself by assisting authors, doing the hands-on work for them, creating outstanding, top quality, often award-winning books.

Ellen serves her national and international client base from her Southern California headquarters. She lives in Los Angeles with her dogs Katy and Kiki, and has created a happy family of professionals who come together to serve authors in putting their best book forward.

PUTTING YOUR BEST BOOK FORWARD

PUTTING YOUR BEST BOOK FORWARD

A BOOK SHEPHERD'S **SECRETS** TO PRODUCING AWARD-WINNING BOOKS THAT SELL

ELLEN REID

LITTLE MOOSE PRESS®

Beverly Hills, CA

Little Moose Press
269 S. Beverly Dr. #1065
Beverly Hills, CA 90212
866-234-0626

First Edition

Printed in the United States of America

Library of Congress Control Number: 2010905568

Publisher's Cataloging-In-Publication

Reid, Ellen.

Putting your best book forward : a book shepherd's secrets to producing award-winning books that sell / Ellen Reid. -- 1st ed. -- Beverly Hills, Calif. : Little Moose Press, c2010.

p. ; cm.

ISBN: 978-0-9841441-3-6

Summary: With over 500,000 books hitting the market every year, how do you make your self-published book stand out? Ellen Reid knows and she shares what she has learned in her stellar career of working with self-published authors to produce their books.

1. Self-publishing--United States. 2. Authors and publishers-- United States. 3. Publishers and publishing--United States. I. Title.

Z285.5 .R45 2010 2010905568
070.5/93--dc22 1006

Front Cover Design: Chris Collins
Author Photo: Marc Cartwright
Interior Design and Layout: Ghislain Viau

This book is dedicated to Dan Poynter, without whom I would never have become a Book Shepherd. My gratitude is boundless... I have found my calling, thanks to you, Dan!

Table of Contents

Acknowledgments xiii

Introduction 1

Chapter 1

Leveling the Playing Field 3

Chapter 2

Indie-pendence Day 13

Chapter 3

Setting Up Your Publishing Company 15

Chapter 4

Little Bo(ok) Peep 19

Chapter 5

Getting Your Lambs in a Row 23

Chapter 6

Getting Your Book Into Bookstores 45

Chapter 7

New Worlds of Possibility 49

Chapter 8

EEEEEE-books 55

Chapter 9
Contests 57

Chapter 10
Questions and Answers 75

Chapter 11
Don't Just Take My Word for It 87

Chapter 12
The Seven Deadliest Mistakes New Authors Often Make 111

Afterword 115

Acknowledgments

Thank you to everyone on the Book Shepherding team... you know who you are. So many wonderfully talented people have helped me over the years; a special thank you goes to Laren Bright, Patricia Bacall, Dotti Albertine, Pamela Guerrieri, Pam Terry, Ghislain Viau, Chris Collins, Andrea Howe, Melanie Rigney and Melissa Flamson. Thanks to everyone at Sir Speedy Whittier, Mike Daniels and everyone at Sheridan Books, Kim Hawley and Craig Landers at Taylor Specialty Books and too many more to mention here. I appreciate you all so much. And to my wonderful clients for trusting me to shepherd their book, thank you! No list of acknowledgments would be complete without thanking my son, Doug, who named my company, Smarketing. Thanks, Doug!

"To love what you do and feel that it matters,
how on earth could anything be more fun?"

— Katherine Graham

Introduction

I work with people who have written a manuscript and want to publish their book—either by creating their own imprint or self-publishing with another company. They have something important to say and want to get their book out into the world. People want to produce books of excellent quality, so the file (cover, interior, copyright page, etc.) is ready to go to print, no matter which way they decide to go. Independent/self-publishing is the only method I know of where writers retain control of the content and creative elements, and keep the lion's share of the profits.

The way to successfully self-publish involves putting together a creative team of experts to produce a book that looks good and is produced according to the accepted practices in the book industry.

My calling is to work with authors who want their book to be as excellent as their message.

There are many good books available that tell you step by step how to produce a book yourself: in particular, my mentor

Dan Poynter's two books: *The Self-Publishing Manuals,* Volumes I and II are the best books to read on the subject, in my opinion. And there are hundreds more. This book will not do that. It is meant to be an overview of the self-publishing process so you can see that it is not only possible, but fun, to start your own publishing company and produce a wonderful book.

Enjoy the ride...

Ellen

Chapter One

Leveling the Playing Field

Decisions, Decisions, Decisions
The Three Publishing Options... and Which Is the Right One for You?

The Author's Wonderful Fairy Tale

Once upon a time there was an author who had a wonderful idea for a book. So the writer went out and found an agent who got him a huge advance from a big publisher. Then he went on Oprah, sold as many books as there are stars in the sky, and lived happily ever after, writing more books, and hiring a fleet of trucks to take his money to the bank.

I know it sounds silly when you put it that way; however, you have no idea how many people I speak with who have some version of this going on in their minds. Okay, maybe not the part about the trucks, but most authors I speak with genuinely believe they have a great book and think they have a shot at getting on Oprah.

While I am all for supporting people in their dreams, let's do some math. Over 500,000 books hit the market in 2009. Let's say only 10 percent of those authors had aspirations of getting on Oprah. That's 50,000 people. Now consider how many authors will actually get on Oprah's show. One a week? 52. Three a week? 156. Out of 50,000? So what are the odds? Pretty slim. But that's just about getting on Oprah. You may have better odds at getting picked up by a publisher. And probably even better odds of getting an agent. The question is whether that's really the best way for you to go.

So let's look at a number of different options you could consider for getting your book published.

Self-Publishing

It's no secret that this is the approach I love. With self-publishing, the author maintains complete control over the entire process. While there are books that will tell you that you can do the job yourself—and you can if you are the kind of person who is excellent in a number of diverse disciplines ranging from graphic design to copywriting (a very different skill than writing a book)—I recommend an alternative method where you hire a team of professionals with experience in each of the several fields that successfully publishing a quality book requires. Here's why.

Your book is your representative. In many cases, your book is what makes your first impression on people. Not ONLY the writing inside the book, but the all-important editing (I could tell you stories about this for hours) and the "window dressing" for the book—the cover design, the title, subtitle, promotional text (about the book, about the author), the interior layout, the paper, the quality of the printing, and more.

These are the things that sell your book and influence people's opinion about whether what you have to say is valuable. Only when these things do a good job of promoting your book will readers start to pay attention to your message.

This comes into play even if you are a known expert in your field—and perhaps it's even more important then. If you have a positive reputation and are respected for what you know, your book must reflect that or it will diminish your stature ... and credibility. Maybe it won't turn off every reader, but how many book sales do you want to throw away because of a less-than-excellent presentation?

Depending on your interest, experience, and skill at managing creative personalities and complex projects, you might manage this all yourself. However, if you already have a job, you don't need yet another more-than-full-time endeavor. For this and many other reasons, I champion the method where the author collaborates with someone who is an expert in the field.

Get an Agent, Go for a Publisher

Even during the best of times, acquiring an agent has been something of a long shot. It is certainly possible, however, it's far from assured, even for a good author with a saleable book topic.

Today, the publishing business is in turmoil. So if you decide to go the large publishing house route, here's what it takes.

First you need to learn what a query letter is. Then you need to write one. A good one. Next you have to research agents to find those representing authors in your genre.

So let's say you do go looking for an agent. A well-known agent shares a great story about the solicitation process. She says, "Authors are always saying they want to send in a proposal. What should I send you? What chapter should I send you?" Then she smiles and shakes her head and says that some people actually send chapter six.

I mention this to show you that getting an agent is not just hit-and-miss. It's a business that requires research and hard work. There is an entire method of making a presentation to a legitimate agent.

Keep in mind that lots of people are calling themselves agents. In this highly competitive marketplace, if you're going to make an impression on a publisher, you need someone with credibility.

Of course, having an agent can sometimes give you entrée into the movie market. If you have an agent with solid connections in the film industry, and if they like your book and think it has possibilities for a film, they can pitch it for that medium.

Should you find an agent willing to represent you, there is a "pitching process" they will take you through. If you are successful, a publisher may pick you up and then the process of actually producing your book will begin. So, getting the agent is just the beginning.

Because the big houses aren't accepting as many books as they used to, it is very difficult to even get an agent to take on an unknown. Unless you are the next J.K. Rowling, for a first-time author, finding representation isn't easy. For now, though, it is still a possibility.

Another reason why I am such a proponent of self-publishing, especially now, is that you are in control of your book at every phase. Dan Poynter always says that once you self-publish, after your book has some buzz and you have done some terrific marketing and people are buying your book, you can sell to a big house.

There are positives and negatives to all types of publishing. On the plus side of traditional publishing, the author doesn't have any up-front expenses and doesn't have to handle any of the bookkeeping, including things like returns.

On the down side, royalties are only a small percentage of the book's sale price. So, it's a tradeoff. And, unless you are a big name author, it's not likely that you are going to get anything for an advance or a lot in the way of promotional support.

Promotional support is an issue because, let's face it, no matter which publishing option you choose, it is not going to be the publisher who sells the book. If a book is going to sell, it will largely be because of you. Plan to spend money for traditional marketing and now, more importantly, Internet marketing. There are many other promotional expenses that you will have to factor in against what you will make in royalties.

Of course, if a big publisher really likes you, it can put a lot of marketing dollars into you and your book, send you out on book signing tours, and do things that a small publisher probably doesn't have deep enough pockets to do. Plus, they have prestige and if they send the book to reviewers like *Publisher's Weekly* or *The New York Times*, there is a good possibility the book will be reviewed. If it is reviewed and you get a good endorsement line or two from the review, that's always wonderful. Having a big house publish you can be prestigious; however, you need to know what your purpose is with your book and decide if the upsides of a big publishing house outweigh the potential downsides.

The biggest downside is the time lag between when they get and accept your manuscript and when the book is published.

Print-On-Demand

Print-On-Demand and short run printing is a development of digital technology and has revolutionized the publishing business. With POD, your book is stored electronically and copies are printed on an as-needed basis.

POD used to have a bad reputation, but it doesn't anymore. Part of what changed is the need for speed and people wanting a way to get their books out, no matter what.

With POD you don't have to warehouse anything and you don't have to spend a lot of money on a huge print run.

There are some good things about Print-On-Demand and a couple of drawbacks. The good news is you can still create your book any way you choose; you can hire the creative team (cover design, copywriter, editors, interior designers, etc.), and then you can send the completed file to the POD company. Do remember, though, that there are several different approaches with POD, from the budget basement approach (where you give them your manuscript and let them do everything from design to cover text) to you paying outside creative talent to do your design and promotional text and having a Print on Demand house do the printing.

You will want to research which companies will allow you to have your own imprint. Some do, and more may crop up as time passes. However, many POD houses put their name on the spine of the book and they therefore become the publisher of record. And the company with the ISBN gets the money first and then pays royalties to the author.

While this does take some time and energy, if you are on a tight budget, POD is a good option. The Internet is brimming with online POD companies that you can compare.

Another plus for POD is that many of them have connections with the big wholesalers. What this means for you is that once your book is printed by a POD house, if someone walks into a bookstore and asks for your book, it's likely that it will show up as available on the store's computer. That doesn't mean it will be on the bookstore shelf; it means that if someone comes in asking for it, the bookstore will be able to order it.

There's also a peripheral benefit for POD books. Since bookstores have the right to return unsold books for a full refund (and that's regardless of the condition they return them in), when someone orders a POD book, a single copy is printed and shipped. So there are rarely returns with POD books; what you sell stays sold, for the most part, unless a customer returns the book because they don't like it. Even so, though, the higher overall profit to you tends to balance this out to some degree.

On the downside to Print-On-Demand publishing, there is the loss of the impulse, or browser's, sale. When a book is readily available, a potential consumer is more inclined to make a quick purchase. To get a POD book from a bookstore, the customer has to know the book exists and specifically ask for it. Then they have to wait until it's printed and shipped. Many readers want to walk out of the store with their book in hand. That isn't going to happen with POD.

When it comes to returns, there is something every author and publisher must understand: returns can turn a rosy sales (and profit) picture into a big disappointment. One of my clients did a big PR push on his own and bookstores ordered a lot of books. He was very successful in getting the books into the stores—which looked great in terms of wholesale sales. But he did not do such a great job of getting the books out of the stores.

What happened was that at some point the stores took their inventory and then shipped all of the unsold books back to the master distributor. That totally turned everything upside down and the anticipated royalties disappeared. When the master distributor deducted the returns from the royalty projections, the self-publisher was lucky that he didn't owe the distributor money.

That's why Print-On-Demand works for a lot of people when it comes to dollars and cents: If somebody orders a book, they send a book. There's rarely an unsold product.

Another issue with POD books is that there may not be as wide a range of paper stock.

Not to get too technical on you, but POD is done on digital presses. You can think of them as huge, complex copy machines. Unlike offset printing, which deals with actual ink on paper.

I was once setting up a book signing at a bookstore for a client and the store sent me an agreement that asked if the book was a Print-On-Demand. They would not have done the event if it was a POD. So that's another piece to factor in when considering this approach.

Bottom line: For authors who really need to get a book into print quickly, POD can be an excellent choice.

Co-Publishing

Co-publishing, or using a subsidy press, involves paying an existing publisher to publish your book under their imprint. They pay some of the expense and you pay some.

They are like a big publishing house in that if they like your book, then they can field a whole team of people to produce it for you.

The thing that's interesting too about all the subsidy and co-publishers is that each has its own approach, and the process is not standard throughout the industry. If you're considering going the co-publishing route, you will want to take the time to listen and to understand what each of them is offering. These excellent companies generally handle the entire bookstore distribution process for you, including warehousing and fulfillment. While you may not have to worry about accounting, it comes at a price. When considering co-publishing, there are a lot of factors that can determine a variety of outcomes for the final product.

With a co-publishing approach, it's like having a big house except you're paying for part of the production costs. And you need to have a clear sense of the business end of the process so you can first understand the packages available and then evaluate the dollars and cents pros and cons.

It's Your Choice

That's a fair overview of the various viable publishing options. The rest of the book will explain what you might encounter and help you avoid costly mistakes.

Chapter Two

Indie-pendence Day

What Is a Self-Publishing House?

Let's start by making an important point: Self-publishing is not what used to be called "vanity publishing."

Self-publishing is when an author produces his or her own book. It is a business.

While vanity press used to be looked down upon by the publishing industry, this is not the case for self-publishing. Today, self-publishers are considered akin to indie filmmakers. They are the heroes who have the vision, ability, and courage to put their ideas and creativity out to the public. And, much like indie filmmakers, the public will recognize quality and reward it with their dollars. That's why I say you must put your best book forward.

Every year the amount of books introduced to the market increases. And the percentage of self-published books is rapidly rising. Even major media are recognizing and acknowledging that self-publishing has become a legitimate and viable business. So, you can see this is a thriving book market. And it is highly competitive. The book business is thriving.

Chapter Three

Setting Up Your Publishing Company

Getting Down to Business

In order to publish your own book, you need to create your own imprint. This is simply a name of a publishing company that you come up with. Some people already have companies and they start a new imprint using the name of their existing company. For example, let's say your company is Smith Consulting. You can easily set up Smith Publishing or Smith Press. You get the picture; there are few rules for coming up with a good imprint name.

It is important to have a mailing address for your publishing company. I suggest using UPS Store or MailBoxes, Etc., in your neighborhood. Choose a place that has an actual address and "suite number." Don't use a PO Box.

Once you have your address, it is important to get a separate telephone number, e-mail address, and Web site.

Some Nuts & Bolts—But Not a Lot

Having established your business presence, you can start signing up for the various registration numbers you will need. Among these are:

ISBN (isbn.org)—International Standard Book Number
LCCN (pcn.loc.gov)—Library of Congress Control Number
PCIP—Publishers Cataloging-in-Publication

There are plenty of good books, like Dan Poynter's Self-Publishing Manual, that can walk you through the steps of getting these things and advise you on how to handle other technicalities you'll encounter. If you don't go the book shepherd or consultant route, I suggest you get one of those books to assist you in getting a good picture of what you need to do.

A Quick Look at the Benefits of Self-Publishing

Self-publishing is the best of all worlds for several reasons:

When you start your own publishing company, you control absolutely everything about the way the book looks and feels because you put a team together, you pay people to do what you want them to do, and you have the final say on everything. You control everything from title, subtitle, and promotional text (back cover and flap text) to cover design, interior page design, even the paper stock.

When you work with book shepherds or book consultants, they will guide you by providing solid information based on their experience and research so you can avoid costly mistakes.

A good advisor will assist you in avoiding poor choices that are based on personal, subjective preferences instead of sound professional experience.

And while you always make the ultimate decisions, you will find that a team of professionals guided by a project leader will take your ideas and produce something that goes far beyond your initial vision. Your job is to write a good book. Their job is to present the book to your market in a way that will support, encourage, and even compel your market to buy it.

Move Faster. With a big publishing house, it could take up to 24–36 months to get a book in print. When you are driving the process, you can have a book in six months or less.

Create Multiple Streams of Income. One of the really great advantages of self-publishing is that once you create your book, you can repurpose your material. You can turn your book into a CD, you can make it available for wireless reading devices, such as the Amazon Kindle, the Apple Ipad, the Barnes & Noble Nook and many more. You can turn it into an electronic download, or you can adapt it into a workbook.

There are a million ways to reinvent your book. If you own the book, you make the choices, and you get to keep the money from each one.

As a self-publisher, you invest in your book, you take responsibility for promoting your book, and you reap the rewards of your work.

And One More Point

When you are a publisher, not only can you publish your own book, but you can publish other people's books. You are a publishing house. You can publish books by others who may want to create a book but don't want to tackle the other things necessary to get it published.

Chapter Four

Little Bo(ok) Peep

What Is a Book Shepherd?

Book Shepherd is a term that was coined by self-publishing guru Dan Poynter years ago to describe a new group of professionals in a burgeoning field. He calls us the godparents of self-publishers and authors. A book shepherd is someone who can guide you through the entire process of creating a book so you're not out there flailing your arms around trying to figure out what to do next.

I think right now there are over around two dozen people who identify themselves as book shepherds, but we all do very different things. One book shepherd is an editor, so when you get her, you get her as a book shepherd with an emphasis on the editing aspect. Another book shepherd was a writer first, so she brings that focus. Yet another is a book designer, and she proceeds from that platform. So it's important to know what each person's primary area of expertise is when selecting a book shepherd.

There's also a question of personality. I always say that book shepherding is like dating: You have to find the right fit with someone. You just have to feel it because it's a pretty intense, and intimate, relationship.

"Your book is your baby and you want to have a midwife who's going to help you birth it so that it has a great chance of growing up well."
—Ellen Reid

Why "Shepherd" Is a Good Description

When I think of a shepherd, I think of someone who's running around chasing sheep who have strayed away from the flock. That's a pretty good image for what managing the production of a book looks like. There are a million details to keep track of and keep in line. Some deal with the creative process, like making sure the cover image of a book represents the message the author is trying to get across, in a way that will stand out against other books of a similar type. Some are executive level details like making sure the creative team is working together harmoniously so you get that special synergy going between them that results in an outstanding book.

Yet other concerns are administrative, like arranging for ISBN, LCCN and other all important numbers, bar codes, and the like. And still others are managerial, like keeping the production schedule on track.

To switch metaphors, I often liken being a book shepherd to being a movie producer. For example, if you wrote a screenplay and hired Steven Spielberg to produce and direct it, you better believe that you're not going to be telling the casting director who to use or the cinematographer what kind of shot to take or the costume director what kind of clothes the characters should wear. You hired Spielberg to do that. And based on his track record, you're going to trust him to get the job done in the very best way possible. Maybe you'll go to him with suggestions or he'll come to you with questions; however, by and large, you're going to go with his call.

That's generally a good analogy to describe the best way to work with a book shepherd.

So Do You Really Need a Book Shepherd?

You may be a wonderful writer who can tell a terrific story or present ideas and techniques with crystal clarity. And maybe you have a pretty good eye for design and a computer program that will do what looks like a pretty good layout. However, that does not automatically mean you can create a great front cover and write the kind of promotional material (back cover and flap text) that will capture a casual browser and transform them into a buyer in the 30 seconds of attention they will give your book. To compete and really put your best book forward, you need professionals.

In most cases, in my experience, authors are not the best people to title their books. Why? Because they are too close to the subject. Their job is to know how to tell their story or present their information, not how to best sell it. So the title, subtitle, back cover, flap text, and even the short author's bio need to be written by someone who is solely focused on selling the best benefits to the author's market. And these benefits may not be what the author considers the key points. Great writers of books are not generally great writers of promo text (which includes every word on the cover of the book, including the title).

One writer called me and asked me to take a look at his book. The first thing that I noticed was that his entire back cover was a bio of him. You might be amazed at how many times I've seen something like that (unless, of course, you've done exactly that with your own book, in which case I guess you wouldn't be amazed).

Browsers want to know what's in the book. They especially want to know, what's in it for them? What's the book about?

The bottom line is that you need objective professionals to help with the back cover copy, then you want to have it laid out properly with a book designer, and you want it all consistent with the front cover and genre.

Chapter Five

Getting Your Lambs in a Row

Breaking Down the Book Shepherd's Tasks

It would be great if there were a nice clean description of what a book shepherd is supposed to do. But, alas, there isn't. When Dan Poynter coined the phrase, it really covered a variety of tasks, and some book shepherds do many or most of them, and others do a couple of them.

This chapter is dedicated to identifying and describing the various tasks you might expect a book shepherd to undertake for you.

Reading Your Book

In order for a book shepherd to direct your creative team, she needs to know what your book is about. A book shepherd also needs to see what shape the manuscript (or book) is in so she can advise you as to whether it would serve your interest to hire an editor, proofreader, or other form of manuscript doctor.

Don't expect a book shepherd to read your manuscript for free. A successful book shepherd will have tons of things to read, both for clients and to keep up with a changing industry. So, if you're not sure you want to hire a particular shepherd, most have a modest flat fee for reading and evaluating your manuscript.

Based on her evaluation, and the relationship you develop with her in this process, you should have a good idea if you'd like to proceed further with that individual. Worst case scenario is that you will end up getting some very useful feedback for a reasonable price.

Assembling the Creative Team

There are three key players in the creative teams I assemble: the copywriter, the cover designer, and the interior designer. Each has an individual role, but with proper coordination among them, a synergy can develop.

The Copywriter

The process starts with the copywriter. The cover designer can't design until he knows the title and subtitle. The back cover and About the Book text also assist the designer in getting a sense of the book.

When I hire a copywriter, he provides a "package" of services that includes the book title, subtitle, back cover text, flap text (or what I call the About the Book—more on this in a minute), and the author's bio. Because we do this as a package, the writer can amortize the preparation time over several elements and provide a better price per element.

A good copywriter will need to read the manuscript in order to accurately write promotional text for it. That can take a great deal of time. If the copywriter had to charge for all that time to do one element, like a title or subtitle, it would add substantially to the cost of that piece. However, with a package, the writer can spread that reading cost over several pieces so the cost of each piece is significantly less.

While this is not intended as a how-to book, I think it will serve you to understand what each of the elements of a book is intended to do, so you can make sure your creative team is providing what you need.

Title. A book's title should stimulate a browser's interest using succinct, compelling words. It can be somewhat descriptive; however, it doesn't need to explain fully what the book is about. With fiction books there is pretty much free reign. You can title a fiction book almost anything that has some relevance to the subject of the book. Self-help, how-to, or other semi-instructional nonfiction books generally work best when it is more directly related to the subject of the book. The short 4-6 word titles are perfect.

Subtitle. The subtitle should explain what the book is about and state or imply a benefit. In other words, the subtitle should give the browser a reason to want to learn more about the book.

Back Cover. The back cover deals with the benefit the reader will gain by reading the book. The back cover helps the browser become a buyer.

Testimonials are great for a back cover because other people can say things about your book that you can't. The best testimonials are from known authorities in your field. However, even an unknown name can make an impactful statement that you can't make yourself.

In addition to testimonials, a well crafted short paragraph or a few lines that highlights the benefits will work well on a back cover.

Flap Text. When you have a dust jacket, flap text should get more into the nitty-gritty of what the book has to offer. For example, let's say your title is Unbelievable Wealth, and your subtitle might be Ten Tips for Doubling Your Investment Income. Then the back cover says that once you read this book you're going to sell all your stocks because you're going to discover an investment strategy that will set you up for retirement in five years.

Before the browser is going to be a buyer, he or she is going to want to know whether you've really got something or whether you're making a bunch of promises you can't fulfill. That's where the flap text comes in. For our hypothetical book, the flap text will need to say something like, "After ten years of rigorous research, the author has proven without a doubt that investing in chinchilla farming is the industry of the future. Her step-by-step guide for choosing the right animals, creating the best environment to produce the thickest pelts, and knowing the best markets to sell them to will put you right smack in the driver's seat to success as a chinchilla farmer."

The trick to good flap text is to tell enough to convince the browser that they will gain substantial amounts of useful information without giving it all away on the flap. Good flap text will convince a browser that they want to know more about the topic.

With fiction books, the trick is to tell enough of the story to draw the reader in to want to know where the story goes and how it turns out.

It's hard for authors to determine the best balance for this. They are simply too close to their subject or their story to know how to give an interested reader just enough to tip the scale so the consumer buys the book. Most often authors want to tell way too much in the promo text.

This explanatory information will generally fill the front flap and may extend onto the back flap. The back flap will also often have an author's short bio, and the author's head shot.

Here's a big secret! When I got into the book shepherding business, I saw early on that most authors were producing trade paperback books. And trade paperback books do not have flaps. Research has shown that bookstore browsers respond pretty much as follows: If the book cover (which includes the title and subtitle) intrigues them, they will pick up a book and read the back cover. If that captures their interest but they're not ready to buy yet, they will read the flaps. Usually that will clinch the deal. If not, they will check out the table of contents.

I realized that we could be losing some of our sales opportunity if there were no flaps. So I came up with the idea of something I call "About the Book." What this does is gives us prime real estate in the book to make the flap text sales pitch and gives us an added opportunity to convince a browser to buy the book.

I have my copywriter compose flap text with an intriguing headline and I put it in the front part of the book. So when a browser has completed reading the back cover and is looking for more information before buying the book, they open the book and look at the first few pages on the way to the table of contents and find compelling text to help convince them.

About the Book text is identical to flap text in content. The only difference is where it appears in the book. I believe including this in a trade paperback can make a great deal of difference in making a sale. And, as an added bonus, I often suggest they use this same text on Web sites and other promotional materials, so my clients get a lot of bang for their buck with it.

About the Author. A good author's bio will be a few lines that highlight why you are qualified to write this book and why the browser would want to know what you have to say. It is an art to write a good author's bio. Because it needs to be short, that makes it all the more important to be densely packed with the right information.

One copywriter I use likes to add a closing personal tidbit about the author that makes the writer human and approachable—someone the browser might like to know.

The Cover Designer

Cover design is a very specialized form of graphic design, much like neurosurgery is a specialized form of medicine. Just as you probably wouldn't go to your general practitioner to reconnect severed nerves, you really don't want to go to a general graphic designer to create your book's cover. More to the point, while you probably can remove a sliver from your finger, you probably wouldn't opt to take out your own appendix; neither would you want to design your own book cover just because you have some proficiency with a page layout program on your computer.

Okay, enough with the medical analogies. The point is, your book's cover is the way your book makes its first impression. If it's not the very best it can be, browsers will not look at it long enough to catch the title or subtitle, and you will have lost a sale.

Here's another thing I've found with professional book designers. Sometimes a client will come to me with a clear picture of their book cover in their mind. Some designers will simply execute that design and the client is happy.

The approach I take with my designers is a little different. We listen to the author's ideas and then the designer and I, and sometimes the copywriter, have what I call a shirt sleeve session. We look at what the book is really about and what imagery might communicate that. We consider what colors work best for the target audience (not just for the author who may simply like a particular color). And we work to come up with a cover that plays off the title and essence of the material so that it grabs attention and, more importantly, motivates interest.

Almost invariably I hear comments that affirm the end result is miles ahead of what the author originally had in mind. This is one of the most dramatic examples of how professionals, and especially a seasoned book shepherd, can contribute to taking a good book idea and transforming it into an outstanding finished book.

In addition to overall design, you may need advice on whether you need to produce a hard cover book with a dust jacket or whether a trade paperback will be just as effective for you. There's also the question of whether your photo will go on the book, either as part of the cover design for a self-help or business book, or in the back flap of a fiction book. If you're going to have a photo in or on the book, make sure it's done by a professional. I have seen the difference between a very good amateur shot and one done by a professional. Believe me, there is a difference and a pro is worth what you pay.

Some designers have experience that will assist you in making the best choices for your book. A good book consultant or book shepherd should be able to expand your vision beyond what you have in mind to what you would have thought of if you could have.

Interior Designer

About two-thirds of my clients provide me with a manuscript that they have produced in Microsoft Word. They have created the pages the same size as a trade paperback (approximately 6 x 9) and they think that they have a page layout that really works. They wonder why I tell them they need to pay for page layout when they have some proficienty with a program on their computer.

And then I show them a professionally laid out page and their jaws drop.

The differences between a professionally done page and one done in Word range from dramatic to subtle. For one thing, page layout computer programs for professionals provide way more control than a generic program like Word. It allows adjusting for tracking and kerning (the space between letters) as well as fine line spacing. While this may sound subtle, it's not.

Along with knowing line lengths that are eye-friendly, appropriate margins, and creating customized page templates, a professional page designer will provide you with interior pages that readers will enjoy reading. This is hugely supportive of getting your message from the page and into your readers' awareness. And it has a subtle influence on browsers who may be leafing through your book trying to decide whether to buy it or not.

Editors

Who Needs An Editor Anyway?

The answer to that question is: Anyone who wants an end product that looks, feels, and reads like a professionally done book. However, keep in mind that there are several kinds of editors, from proofreaders who will make sure there are no typos or punctuation errors, to content editors who will function almost like a ghostwriter to make sure your message is presented clearly and well. Depending on how well you write, you may need an editor, or multiple editors for various stages of the production, to fulfill a number of functions for you.

When I speak with writers—or people who have great ideas but don't think they are writers—I always tell them that the most important thing is to get their ideas down on paper, even if it's just stream of consciousness. They don't need to edit it too deeply because, depending on their budget and their skill, they can have an editor take what they've got and turn it into a manuscript that can be reworked into a respectable book.

Before you turn your nose up at the idea, let me assure you that you have absolutely no idea how many popular books, right up to some best sellers, were not written by the person whose name or picture is on the cover. A successful speaker or someone who is involved in important research may have excellent ideas or tools and techniques but lack the skill of a professional writer or the time necessary to craft a top-notch book. It is totally legitimate for such figures to hire professionals who can write the book they would write, just as they would write it, if they had the time or writing talent.

Big publishing houses have editors on staff and will automatically give a manuscript to an editor. Seasoned writers expect this and many will tell you that a good editor is worth his weight in diamonds. So regardless of your writing skill, you can have a well written book if you hire a good editor.

Copyediting, Production Proofreading, Printer Proofs

Copyediting. Although definitions of copyediting are somewhat fluid, and the workflow can vary from project to project, the overall processes, tools, and tasks can be generally described as follows.

1. Description. The manuscript will be edited for clarity, correctness, consistency, and coherency. Copyediting is considered "complete" after the Author has reviewed and approved the copyedited manuscript, and the Editor has prepared the manuscript for the book designer.

2. Process. The Editor will make corrections and queries using Word's Track Changes function, and work with the Author to finalize the manuscript. Copyediting includes two complete passes through the manuscript. On the second pass, the Editor will perform a manuscript "clean up" (including adding new Author material and incorporating Author's responses to Editor's queries) prior to handoff to the book designer.

3. Levels of Editing. Copyediting may be performed at a light, medium, or heavy level. See attached "Levels of Editing" for further information.

4. Components of Copyediting.

   a. Style sheet. Create manuscript style sheet to ensure consistency. The style sheet covers elements such as mechanics (spelling, capitalization, etc.), formatting (references, headings) and documentation (bibliography, endnotes).

b. Mechanical editing. Correct errors in capitalization, punctuation, spelling, etc.

c. Language editing. Check for language problems (grammar, usage, etc.).

d. Correlating parts. Check contents page against chapters, etc.

e. Content editing. Make note of and/or correct internal inconsistencies, discrepancies, factual errors, faulty organization, or gaps in logic.

f. Permissions. Note any permissions that Author may be required to obtain.

g. Cover text. Proofread cover/jacket text, as requested.

h. Ready manuscript for designer. Prepare manuscript for layout by book designer: ensure correct spacing after punctuation, and clean up formatting, etc., per designer specs. Provide manuscript style sheet to designer.

About Proofreading

Proofreading is usually defined as the process of comparing a newer against an older (or "control") version of a document. Proofing without a control document is sometimes known as "blind" or "cold" proofreading. In any event, proofreading should be performed on a printout rather than electronically. Typos and other errors, especially those not picked up by spell check, may be hard to spot on-screen but are usually quite obvious on paper.

If an author asks that someone "just proofread" a manuscript, bear in mind that while copyediting includes proofreading, proofreading does not include any editing. One instance where "just proofreading" may be desirable is when a manuscript has already been copyedited, but a review by a fresh set of eyes is highly desirable because of a complex, long, or otherwise difficult manuscript. Another reason to request a straightforward proofreading is if the author is an excellent self-editor and has a strong grasp of the copyediting function.

Production Proofreading. After the book designer has laid out the book's interior using the copyedited manuscript, Editor will check the print-ready manuscript for errors that may have been introduced during the design process. Production proofreading includes:

1. Manuscript. Compare designer's book printout against copyedited manuscript:

    a. Check first and last word of each paragraph and overall paragraph size.

    b. Make sure paragraph breaks are consistent with original.

    c. Ensure that no text or other elements are missing.

2. Pagination:

    a. Check that page numbers of all sections begin where they should; check that roman and arabic numerals are correctly placed.

    b. Ensure sequential page numbering.

3. Table of Contents. Compare Contents against the book itself:

    a. Check correctness of chapter titles, including spelling and exact wording.

    b. Check (cross-reference) page numbers.

    c. Check that all elements/sections of the book are represented.

4. Page headers/footers:

    a. Check headers/footers against Contents and chapter openers, including spelling and exact wording of chapter titles.

    b. Make sure headers/footers are the same within each chapter.

    c. Check consistency of formatting among all headers/footers.

    d. If chapter/section openers have different headers/footers, make sure every chapter/section opener follows the style (for example, no folio or header/footer on opener page).

5. Chapter openers:

   a. Make sure chapter opener style is consistent on all chapter openers, including graphics, spacing, spelling, wording, formatting, etc.

   b. Make sure first paragraph style is consistent on all chapter openers, including capitalization, use of drop caps, indentation, etc.

6. Indentation:

   a. Check manuscript for extra spaces before paragraphs.

   b. Make sure all paragraphs are indented correctly and consistently.

7. Italics:

   a. Highlight italics in the manuscript and match them up with the book file, ensuring all are present (the italics can get dropped when importing the manuscript into the graphic design software).

8. Graphics:

   a. Check for consistency within recurring graphics such as section break markers, including position, characters or symbols, size, and style.

   b. Check for consistency in spacing, style, etc., on graphics such as tables, charts, captions, and so forth.

   c. Punctuation marks (quotation marks, apostrophes, en and em dashes): Ensure consistent use of typewriter or typeset characters, per style sheet.

9. Bad breaks and other anomalies. Scan line by line for:

    a. Awkward widows or orphans.

    b. Overly loose or tight text/character spacing.

    c. Bad word breaks (e.g., "could–n't).

    d. Erroneous bad breaks in middle of line, etc.

    e. Consistency in justification of text.

    f. Other erroneous symbols or foreign fonts that have not converted correctly.

All errors are noted and a marked-up manuscript and/or list of corrections is sent to the designer. The designer inputs the changes, and then a new file is returned to the copyeditor, who checks to ensure that all corrections were made. Since the designer may inadvertently skip some corrections or introduce new errors during the revision process, it may take two or more rounds of checking before all corrections have been input and errors eliminated.

Once the designer's file is considered final, it is ready for the printer. The proofreader should always have the final look at the actual file to be sent to the printer, simply because any time a file is edited using graphic design software, an error can be introduced.

Printer Proofs. Checking the printer proofs is the final proofreading stage before the book is published. This proof is the last chance for everyone to review the typeset book, as well as the point at which the author is asked to give final approval to print. The proofreader must carefully check the printer proof to make sure the printer didn't introduce any errors during typesetting (e.g., dropping text or graphic elements). The proofreader also checks the overall print quality to ensure that the book is clean and ready to go.

Proofing printer proofs includes:

1. Compare the printer proofs to the final printout supplied by the book designer; ensure all text and graphics are accounted for and correctly laid out.

2. Check pagination.

3. Check font quality throughout.

4. Check quality of all graphic elements, including illustrations or photos.

5. Visually scan for hickeys, dirt, or other unwanted marks.

6. Perform final check of ISBN and Contents page numbers.

Author's note: This is a compilation of information I have received from editors over the years. If it sounds like you, let me know!

The Process

When I work with a client, the first thing we do is evaluate the author's creative needs. Once I present my perspective, I begin reviewing the creative professionals I have worked with. I consider the experience and personality of each one in the context of my client's personality and working style, and what their needs are.

When I arrive at the team I think will serve best, I can direct the client to each person's Web site or provide samples of their work if a client wants to know more about each of the professional's backgrounds.

Additional Lost Sheep the Book Shepherd Tends

Creating a solid team is the tip of the iceberg of what I do as a book shepherd. Let's not forget the whole raft of things you need to know.

Setting Up Your Publishing Company

Your book is not going to get serious attention from distributors or bookstores if it looks like a one-time effort. You know the value of your message or the excellence of your story; however, that's not a distributor's main concern. They are looking at the business end of things. You need to present your book as being published by a company that will do what it takes to be viable in the industry.

Branding is one element that establishes a reputation. You need someone who can design your logo so it works on a book cover, spine, and then handle the myriad details required to put your book into the control publishing system. These include getting an ISBN number, a Library of Congress number, and countless other details.

Can you learn how to do all these things? Absolutely. Is it worth your time and effort? That's the real question. If you think it's really not worth it to you to try to become an expert in these specialized areas, what do you do?

You could just go out and hire a consultant who would either walk you through the steps of setting yourself up as an independent publisher or actually handle them for you. That really works for some people.

In a sense, that's like deciding to build a house and hiring a carpenter, a plumber, and an electrician, telling them what you want your house to look like, and letting them have at it. You will very possibly get a house that will keep the rain out and that will not electrocute you when you flip the light switch.

But think of what happens when you have an idea for a house and you go to an architect. You tell him or her your vision, he or she comes up with some designs, and you pick one that's just what you wanted—only it's better because they know how to put things together in a way that a non-professional doesn't.

Then the architect not only assembles a team, but guides them every step of the way, making sure the job is not only done, but done right; that the electricity works in conjunction with the plumbing, the windows don't stick, and everything works together.

The Bigger Picture

When a big company has a big budget and is ready to hit the market, they go to an advertising agency and say, "I've got a half a million dollar budget and I have a new shoe or new computer. Come up with a campaign." So the agency pulls from its staff of graphic designers, copywriters, and so on and produces a campaign. Of course, the agency has those people at their beck and call because all those people are on the payroll.

Most authors and indie publishers don't have the luxury of that kind of budget. Nonetheless, it does serve them to take the long view if they want to make a real business out of their book. And that means doing more than just getting the book into print.

Here's an example of what I mean by getting the bigger picture. A few years ago I met an author at one of Dan Poynter's seminars. He's a six foot five good looking guy who happens to be a pastor from a small town in Connecticut. He had written a book of really excellent short stories called A Christmas Dozen and he was billing himself as "the Christmas Story Pastor," which was a nickname he had picked up along the way.

We explored working together and he said, "Look, I don't want to just be a pastor. I really want my books to get out there."

So, I pulled in a copywriter who I knew had a pretty diverse background in advertising and we read Steve's books. They were wonderful, heartwarming, Chicken Soup kind of stories. (In fact, one of his stories had been included in *Chicken Soup for the Single's Soul.*) They were not religious-type stories, so we recognized that we needed to broaden Steve's reach because we were concerned non-religious people would not buy a book from a pastor—or at least they might read something into the label that wasn't accurate.

Because Steve's stories were so heartwarming, we re-titled the book Christmas Stories To Warm The Heart and we came up with a sort of branding/tag line for Steve: Story Teller of the Heart.

When we presented this to Steve, he said, "That's me! I am the story teller of the heart!" Interestingly, Steve also wrote fantastic horror stories. So we subtitled that collection Stories to Chill the Heart.

Now, in Steve's case, we were able to provide even more than the written materials and design.

I haven't seen Steve in years, but he calls me from time to time just to touch base. During one of his earliest calls I asked him how he was selling the books besides in bookstores. He said he would go to craft fairs in the summertime. These were largely outdoor events where people have booths at which they sell their products.

I got a strange picture in my mind and asked him what he wore—that is, how did he present himself? He said he usually wore bermuda short and sandals—sometimes with socks as well.

I asked if he had a poster of the book on the table and he said no, he never really put much thought into it. People just sort of show up, set up their tables, and kick back. So, I told him how to put his table together and I also said, "I want you to go buy a pair of khaki pants, a Gucci type belt with the double G's, a beautiful Ralph Lauren type polo shirt, a navy blazer, and Docksiders."

He said, "Why? It's hot! I don't think I want to do that."

I said, "Because you are an author now. You don't want to look like everybody else. You want to look like a successful author."

Long story short, he took my advice. And then he called me. He said, "I can't believe it! I sold more books than I have ever sold at any show and people treated me with such respect. They never treated me like that before!"

Duh!

I don't do this for all my clients, and probably most consultants and shepherds don't do it at all. However, I mention this so you get a sense of how far the book business can reach into your life.

There's a lot to it. How does a small independent publisher really compete when you think about it? The foundation must be laid. Part of creating that quality product comes from working with professionals who care about your project and who will invest time in the details.

Chapter Six

Getting Your Book Into Bookstores

A Bird's-eye View of Wholesale Book Distribution

Getting Your Book Into People's Hands

If you're approaching your book as a business, then there are important things you need to know in addition to how to get your best book produced to promote sales.

The following chapters are intended to give you an overview of various marketing aspects, along with helpful insights into how you can successfully handle the promotional aspect of book publishing.

Presuming you have prepared your book to conform to industry requirements, you have a shot at getting into the major bookstore chains. However, the big guys won't talk directly to you, so you need a distributor. Here's the good news: Because indie publishing is taking off the major distributors are much more inclined to take you on. You must get your book listed in the two biggest wholesalers in the industry, Ingram and Baker & Taylor.

While being in bookstores may sound like a good thing, it has its upsides and its downsides. On the upside, if people come into a bookstore asking for your book, it will show up on the store's computer and they can order it. You want bookstore clerks to say, "Oh yes! This book is in our database. We might not have it on the shelf, but we can get it for you."

The key, really, is getting listed in the bookstore's system. In fact, once you are listed you can go out and market your little heart out and never worry that people aren't going to be able to buy books at their local Barnes and Noble or any bookstore.

The other upside of being in a bookstore is... there is no other upside.

There are really a lot of ways to have a bookstore presence. I recommend getting on Amazon and the other dot-coms: Borders.com, Barnes&Noble.com, Books-A-Million.com. That's where a lot of people go to get their books—online.

The Master Distributor Approach

One approach is to present your book to a master distributor. They will take care of everything for you and get you into all the wholesalers, including handling all your online and digital distribution. This is an excellent opportunity for authors with a "platform" and a budget to print larger quantities of books. Some master distributors have had *New York Times* best selling books due to their efforts.

The bottom line is: Get listed, get listed, get listed. Then go out and do all kinds of marketing—creative and traditional—to increase public awareness of your book.

Chapter Seven

New Worlds of Possibility

The Internet and Why You MUST Be Familiar with It

There is no denying it, we live in a consistently changing world. The Internet is the new mall, marketplace, superstore. It has taken on a major role in the marketing and promoting of everything, including, and maybe especially, books.

Some people think that all you have to do to sell your book is put up a pretty site showing your book's cover, a picture of the author, some sell text, and maybe some testimonials. That might have been adequate at one time, but not anymore.

Just having a pretty site doesn't work. A site with ever changing audio, video, blogs, and much more does. There are some really good programs for creating Web sites today, and you can put up a professional-looking site yourself if you want to. That's great.

You can hire a professional web designer...always a great idea and now you can create your own WordPress blog site. These sites can be created by you, or by a professional but you can do your own updates, which is very important. Now you don't have to have a lot of technical knowledge to create your own Web site and it's inexpensive as well.

To compete in today's Internet market, you must be able to do e-commerce, post videos, and create a blog, to name just a few things an effective site needs to do. And that doesn't even begin to take into account maximizing your Web search performance.

I recently had a client who said he didn't like the sites that only filled the middle of the screen. He wanted a site that filled the whole monitor. Had he created a Web site, that's what he would have produced. He probably would have been happy with it and gotten lots of oohs and ahs from his wife and friends. And all the while he would have been in blissful ignorance that some Web site browsers simply don't support full-screen sites. The result of his decision could have cost him a lot of potential viewers.

Selecting a Web Designer

In selecting a Web designer, especially for authors, it's important to choose one who understands the book business. I have a client who asked me to call a Web designer that he happened to find in his hometown. I had a discussion with her and she showed me a bunch of samples. After admiring her very nicely done design work, I asked if she had ever done a book site. She said she hadn't and suggested I send her some sites and she'd copy them.

I had to explain that I didn't just want to copy a look; I also needed to capture the functionality.

When you hire a Web designer today, you really want a marketer who will do research on the genre as well. Where you used to be lucky if you found a designer who had enough technical knowledge to make your site download in less than two minutes, today you need a marketer who can anticipate what you will need your site to do and be able to deliver one that does it all. And a site that's expandable when the next Internet innovation shows up (like in a month).

Getting a capable, strong marketing team to not only work on the book, but to work on the Web site presence and work with the designers, is absolutely critical. Web sites today need more than nice design and eye-catching pictures. In the ever-evolving world of Web sites, your site needs to be active.

For example, if you are a speaker and you have a video clip of yourself speaking, you can put that up there. You want to tell the designer you want to have that and it's got to go on YouTube.

What I've said about writing promotional text and doing book design is also true for Web sites: The author is too close to the subject to understand what will sell.

What's more, it's not enough to have well-done elements. To be truly successful you need well-done elements that work together. It is the synergy of all the pieces, from the book design, sell text, promotional materials, Web site, and other Internet marketing elements (like social networking sites), that sets the great apart from the merely good.

Elements of a Web Site

Design

Photos. Along with a professional, high quality, high resolution author picture, adding other photos of the author at live speaking engagements is another good way to appeal to online viewers.

One client of mine took a bunch of pictures and she said to the guy who was hosting the site, "Here are thirty pictures. Put them all up and some of them are duplicates so be sure you edit down some of the photos." The creative decisions are the responsibility of the Web designer, not the host. I like to have a gallery section on my clients' Web sites because people like to see who was at the event if it's a book signing or whatever. You don't have to have a hundred of them. Just a few, just a taste. That's all that really matters, and then if there are any credits to be given, you can state those in the captions.

Videos. The importance of a well done video hit home with me a while back when I was working with a Web designer I've used for years. She was a young, very creative woman. She was terrific and quite talented. She's also a photographer and a videographer.

I had her come to a book signing of one of my clients, and a reporter from the local newspaper interviewed the author. My videographer caught the whole event, which, on the surface, was terrific.

However, before she did anything, I wanted to review the footage she had because I don't know what the author had said and I wanted to be sure she didn't say anything she didn't want on video.

So, what this designer did was put the whole video up on YouTube so I could see it. Which was great. Except that not only could I see it, but everyone in the universe could see it. When I looked at it, I was aghast because the author had said some things that would absolutely not be appropriate.

I had to send the designer an SOS e-mail to take it down until I could review it, recommend edits, and get it in shape so it would support the author's message and branding.

While videos are a great way to personally relate to the viewers, make sure it's edited for content before it goes public.

You can now use Camtasia and use your iphone or flip video to film your own videos so this doesn't happen to you. again, control your own site.

Book Trailers. For many years I have been seeking out somebody to produce book trailers, as I really think trailers are a big asset on an author's Web site.

There are several important steps to creating a winning book trailer. First, crafting a good book trailer requires reading the book. So you send them the book, they read the whole thing, and then they'll capture the storyline or essential points in the trailer.

Social Networking. The Internet is fluid. It's beautiful. Not to mention the social networking. People are hiring experts to help them with social networking because authors generally don't know how to do it and they don't want to do it; but that's the hard part—the learning curve—in all of this. We have to learn it and do it!

Chapter Eight

EEEEEE-books

Where the Rubber Meets the Road... Or the Ink Meets the Paper... Or Not

Here's the question of the hour: Are print books a thing of the past? Here's the answer: No way. Books will never disappear. Ebook is an addition, not a substitute for physical print books.

Plan to have your book available in all e-book formats; Amazon's Kindle, Barnes & Noble's Nook, the ipad, the iphone and the Sony ebook reader and many more. This is a big part of the future of the book industry. And here's some good news on that front: Once you have your book designed and laid out for printing, it's relatively simple to turn that file into one that will work for an e-book. And once you have an e-book file, your e-book can be purchased and downloaded from your Web site, from Amazon, or pretty much anywhere.

From your Web site, there are basically three ways to market e-books. One is to offer them free. People who want your book just download it and, since it's free, you don't have to worry about losing money if it's forwarded to others. The reason you might want to give away your e-book is if it's the precursor to selling something else, like a product or service.

The second approach is to charge a minimal amount of money. You can recoup your costs and figure that at a low cost you will do more volume. With this approach you also wouldn't worry much about it being shared with others.

If you do want to sell your e-book on your Web site, be sure to have it encrypted.

The Bottom Line on E-books

Whether you decide to go with an e-book or not is up to you. However, if you do go that way, my strong suggestion is to do that in addition to a print book. Get your book on Kindle, on Smashwords and new Apple iPad and any new e-book readers that come down the pipe. This is the future!

Chapter Nine

Contests

An Interesting Way to Generate Buzz for Your Book

I sponsor contests for books. I enjoy these contests because I want to acknowledge and draw attention to those indie authors who really do it right... who really put their best book forward!

My clients can't enter my contests; however, there are plenty of other contests they can enter.

I feel it's really beneficial for publishers to submit their books for awards. Being able to say you are an award-winning author or that yours is an award-winning book makes a very positive impression on readers and has a lot of impact.

Do you have a shot at winning? If your book is well done, you have a better chance than you might think because most contests have many categories for entries. So you're not always competing against all the books printed in a certain year—you might only be competing with books in your genre. Or you can enter for book design or cover text, if you think your book is particularly strong in those areas.

I know from my clients who have won various contests that there is something special and personally gratifying in putting an award sticker on your book.

And speaking of contests...

The following section presents a variety of book covers we have created. Many of the covers in this section are award winners.